Hi and thank you for choosing my book!

Adrian K.

This coloring book belongs:

____

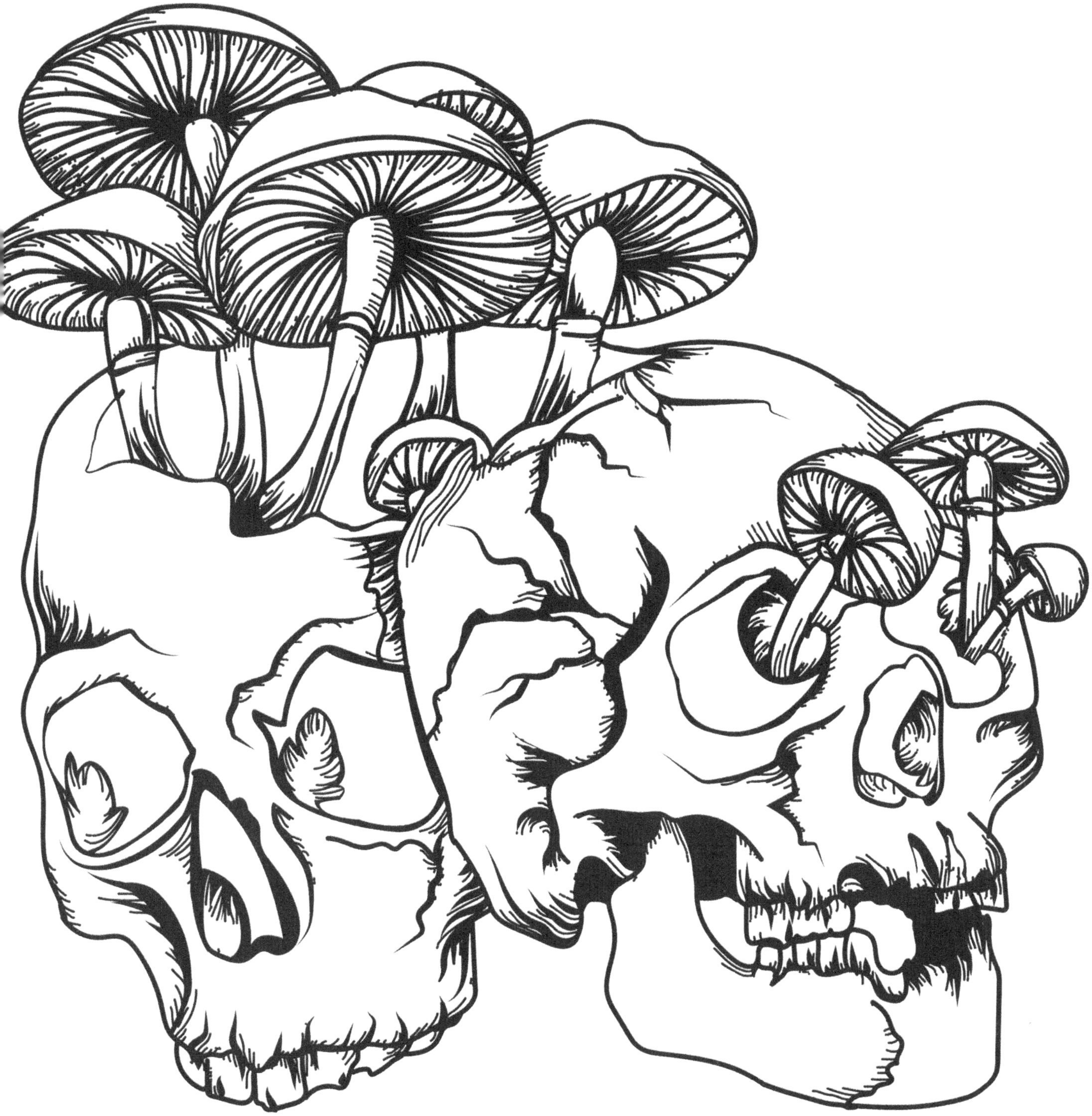

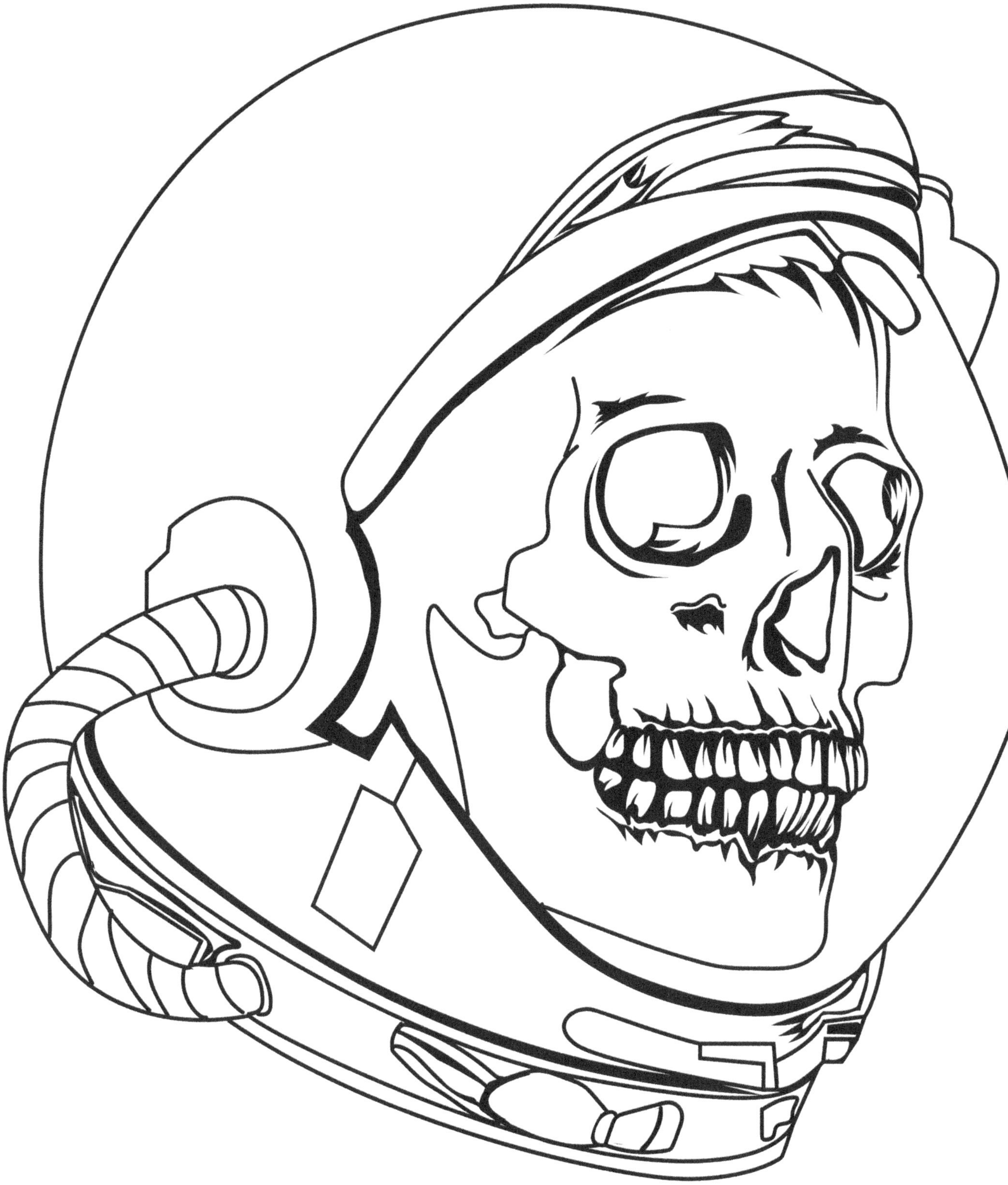

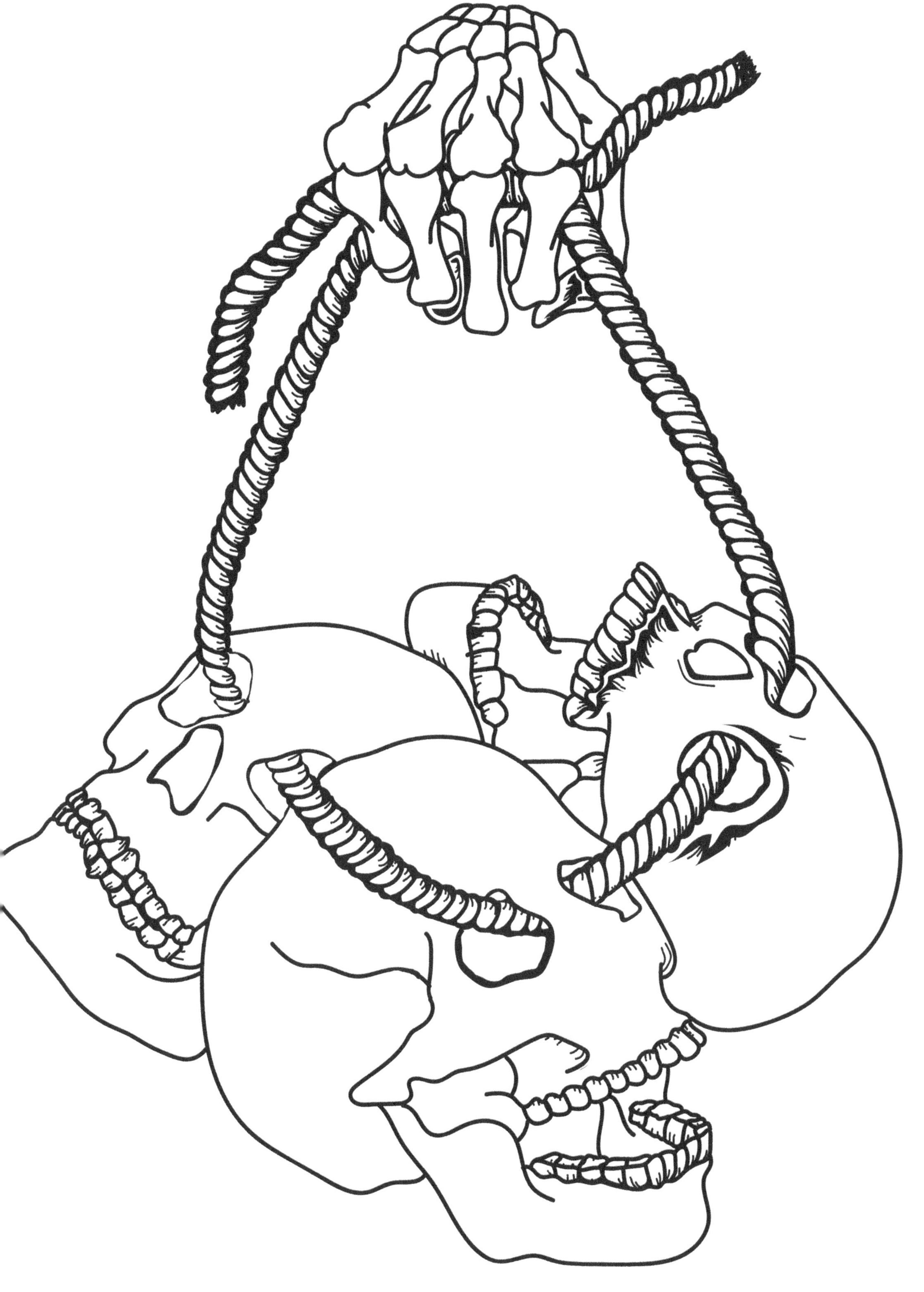

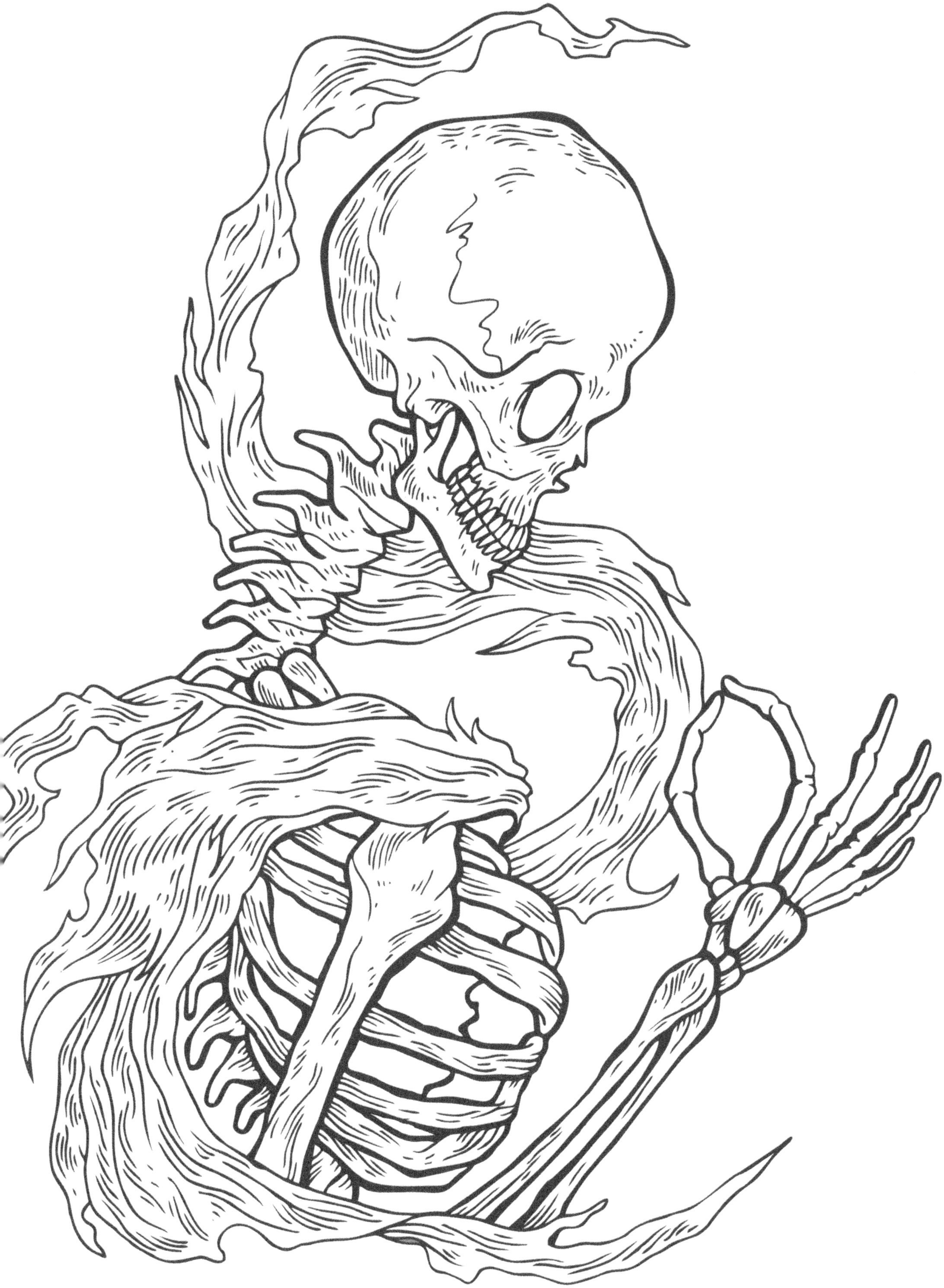

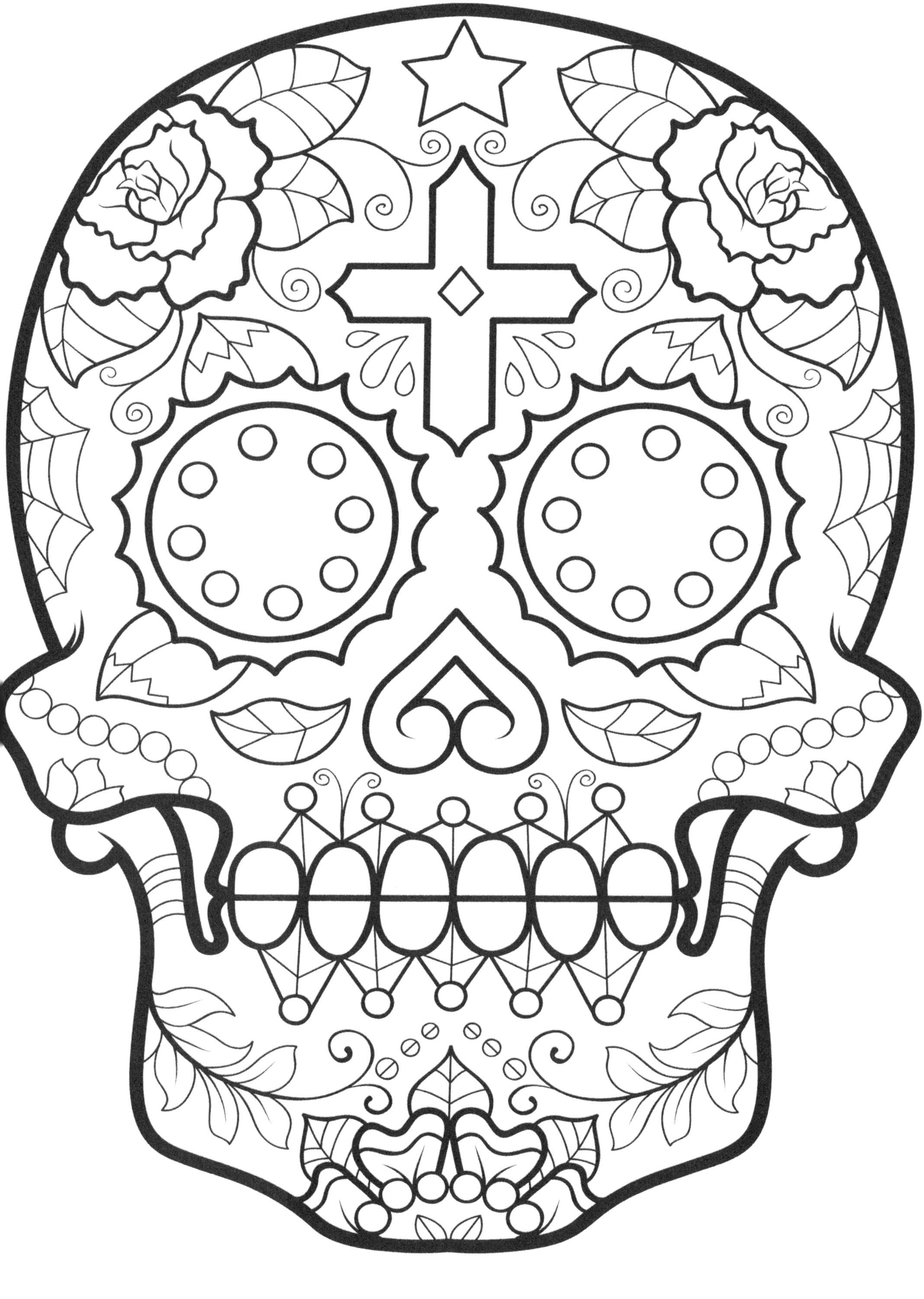

1

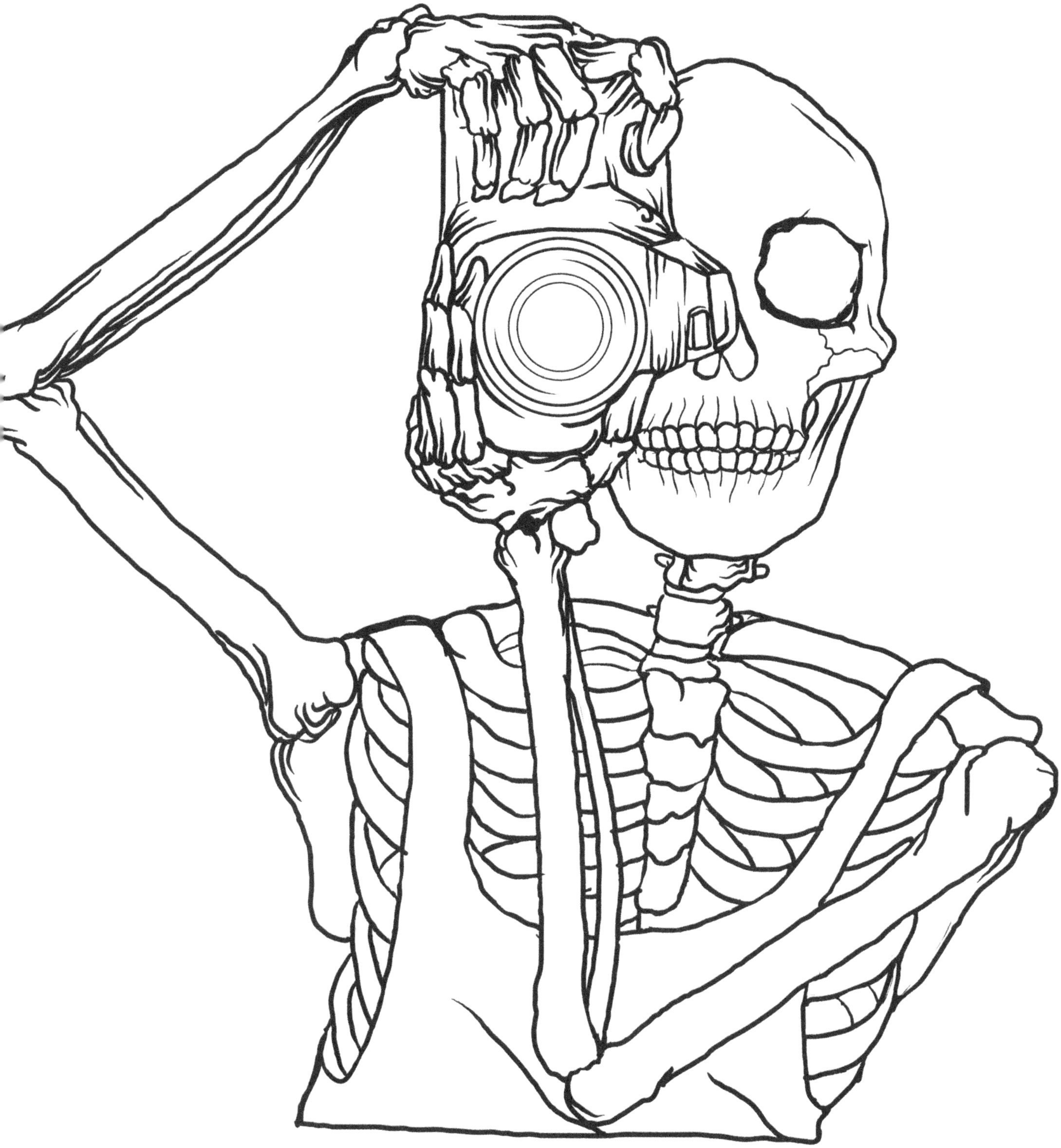

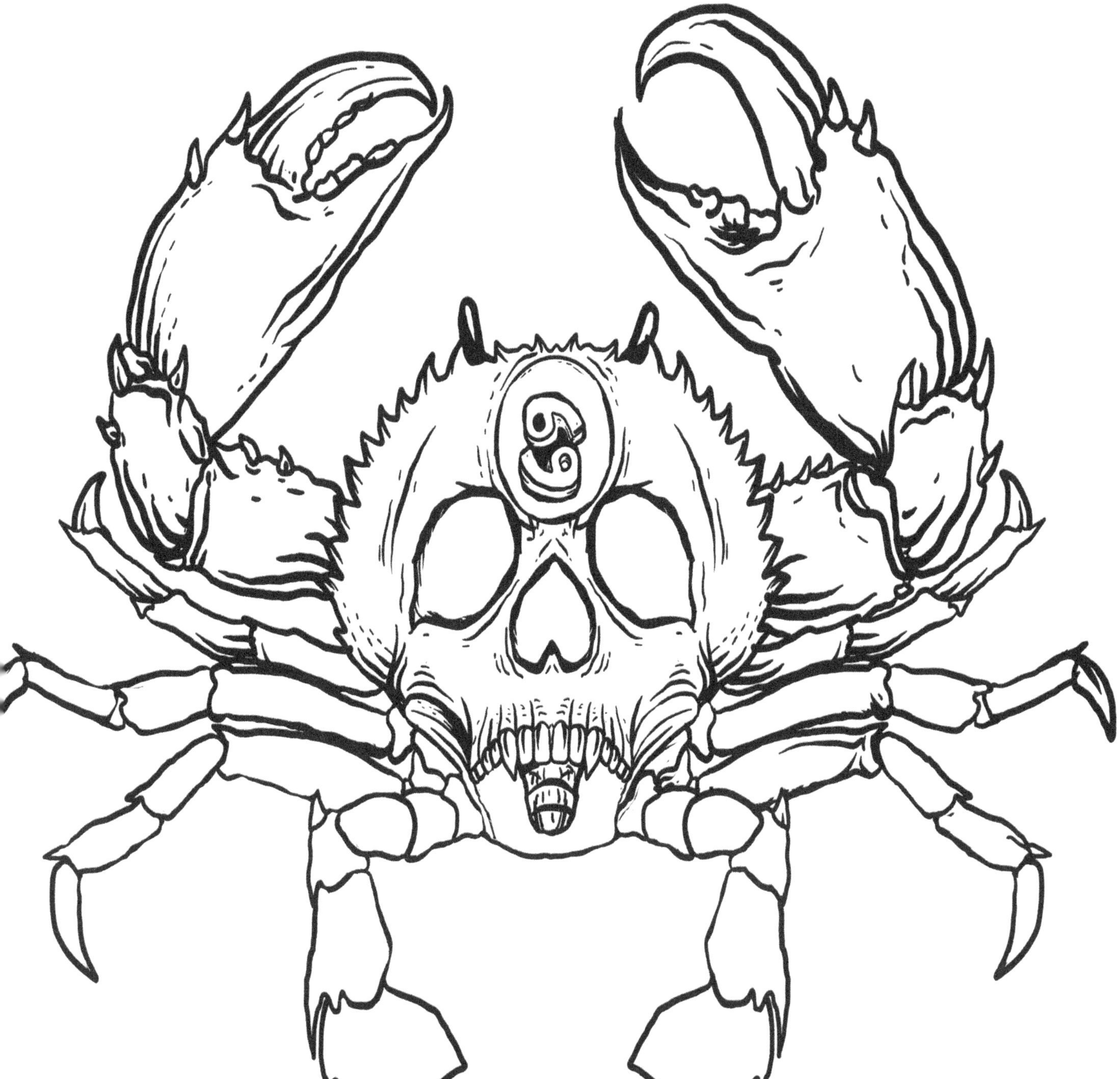

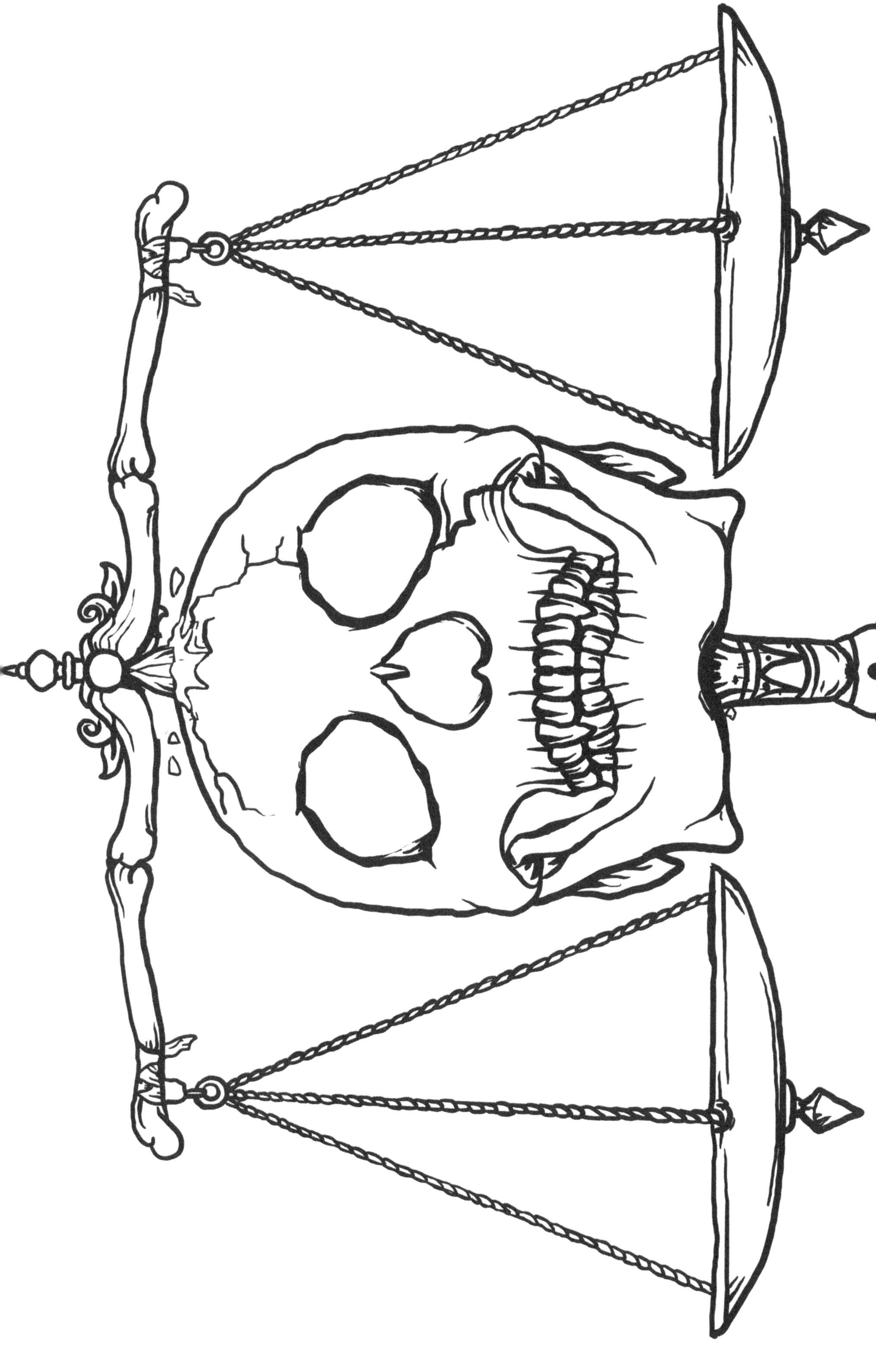

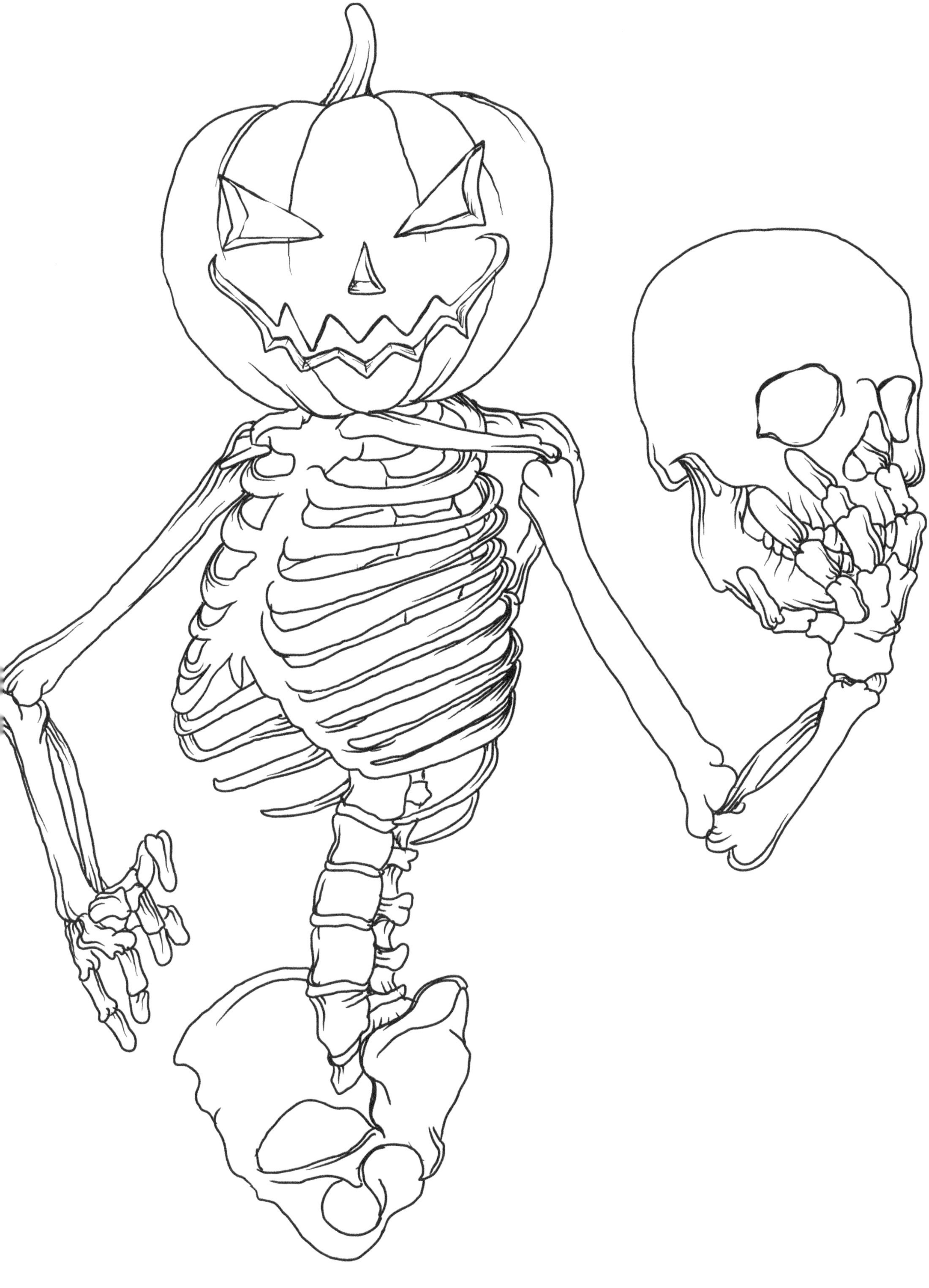

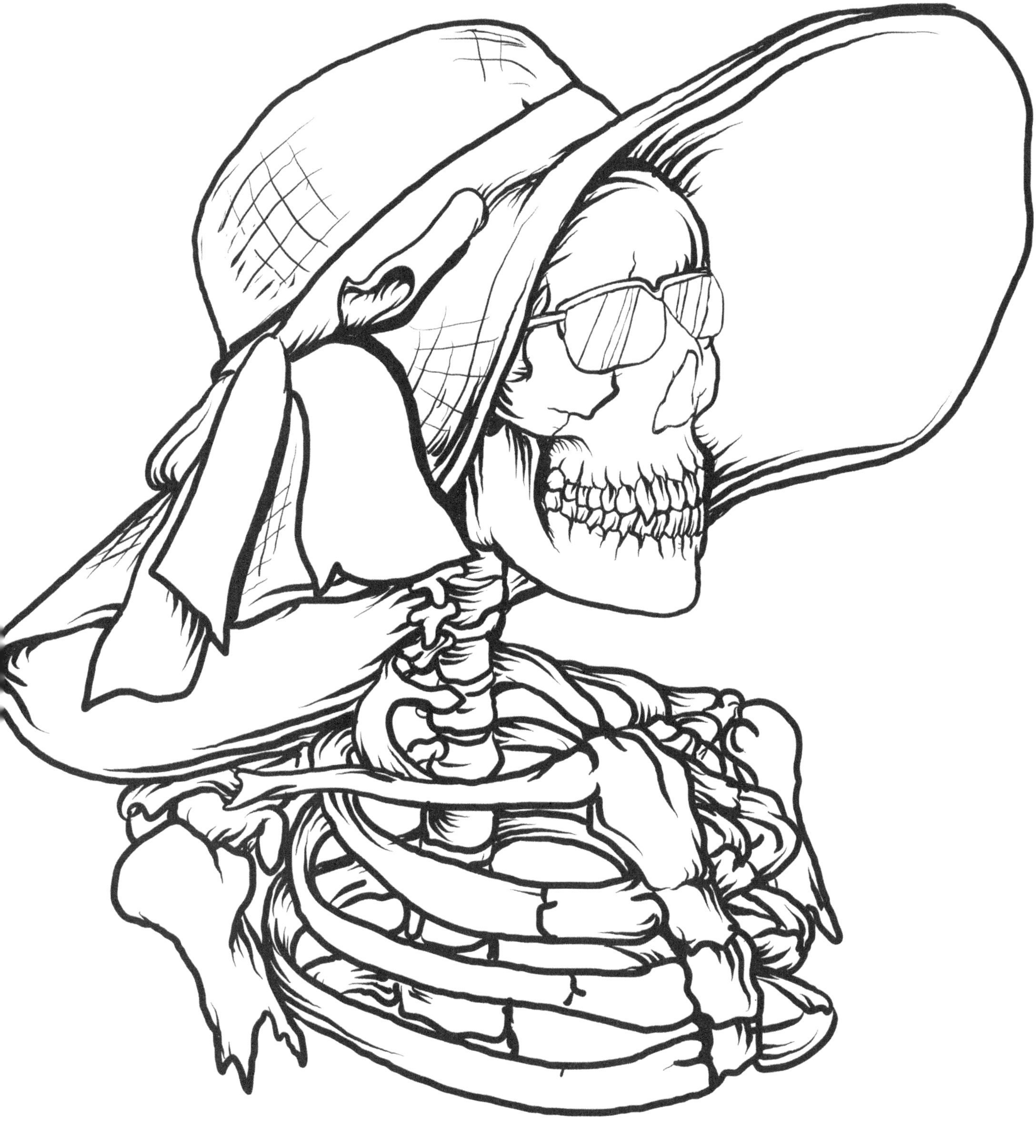

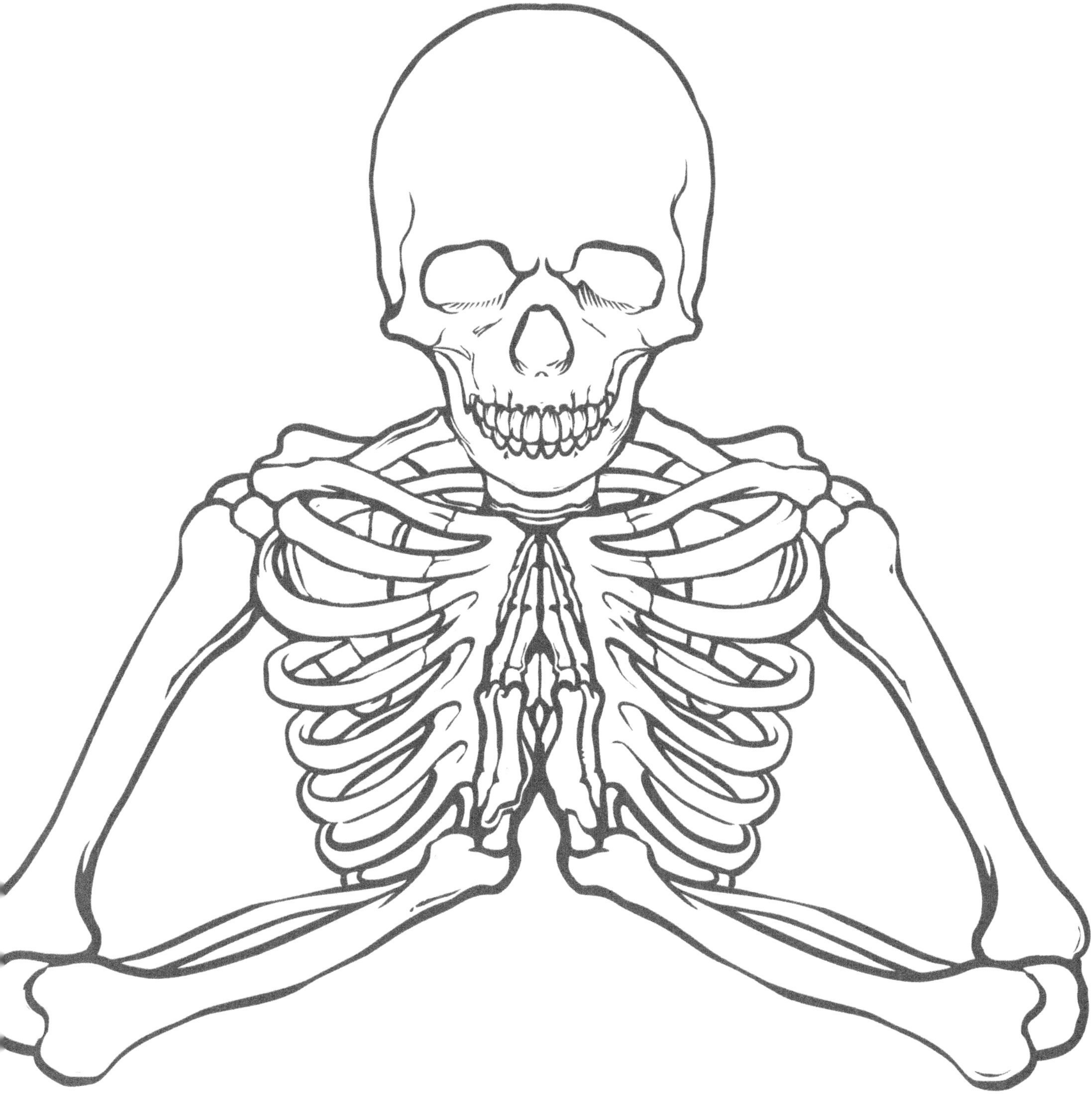

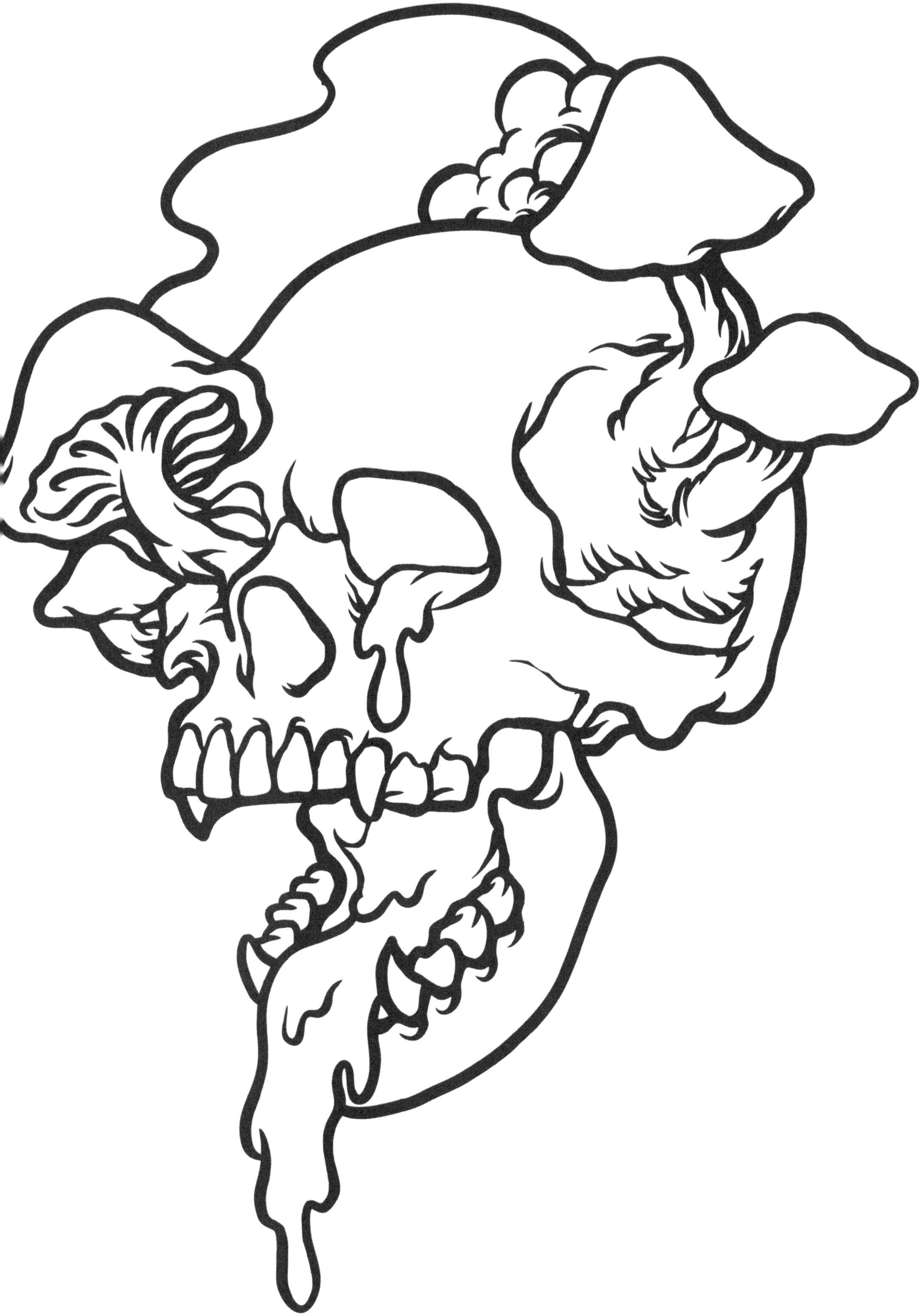

Made in the USA
Monee, IL
18 August 2022

11884404R00070